You are about to read the coolest History series ever written.

"Make History Wavy again"

THE INDUS VALLEY CIVILIZATION

Discovering the Mysterious and Advanced Early Civilization

The Indus Valley Civilization

THE INDUS VALLEY CIVILIZATION

Copyright © 2024 What The History

No part of this publication may be reproduced, stored in a retrieval system, or transmitted in any form or by any means, electronic, mechanical, photocopying, recording, or otherwise, without the prior written permission of the publisher.

Printed in the United States of America

First Edition: 2024

This copyright page includes the necessary copyright notice, permissions request information, acknowledgments for the cover design, interior design, and editing, as well as the details of the first edition.

www.littlebiggiant.com

Disclaimer: This book is a work of non-fiction and is intended for informational and educational purposes only. The names in this biography are trademarks of their respective owners. This book is not affiliated with, endorsed by, or sponsored by any of these trademark holders. The use of these names is intended solely to provide context and historical reference.

The author makes no claims to ownership of any trademarks or copyrights associated with the names and likenesses of the individuals referenced in this book. Any opinions expressed in this book are those of the author and do not reflect the views of any wrestling promotion or trademark holder.

Introduction

The Indus Valley Civilization was like, super advanced, way back in the day, around 2500 BCE. Imagine a place where people had their own cool cities, like Harappa and Mohenjo-Daro, with streets that were all planned out and stuff. They even had these rad drainage systems that were better than some today! But here's the kicker: nobody really knows why this civilization just kinda vanished. Was it climate change? Invaders? Or did they just peace out? It's like a real-life mystery waiting to be solved, and the clues are buried under the sands of time. So, what really happened to these ancient peeps? The answers are out there, just waiting to be uncovered!

THE INDUS VALLEY CIVILIZATION

Table of Contents

Table of Contents **8**
Chapter 1 .... **11**
The Mysterious Beginnings of the Indus Valley Civilization 11
Chapter 2 .... **21**
Amazing Cities: The Urban Planning of Harappa and Mohenjo-Daro 21
Chapter 3 .... **30**
The Great Bath: An Ancient Wonder of Hygiene and Ritual 30
Chapter 4 .... **40**
Writing Without Words: The Indus Script and Its Secrets 40
Chapter 5 .... **50**
Trade and Travel: How the Indus Valley Connected the World 50
Chapter 6 .... **60**
The Art of Living: Crafts, Jewelry, and Toys of the Indus People 60

Chapter 7..**68**
Farming Innovations: The Agricultural Techniques of the Indus Valley..68
Chapter 8..**77**
Religion and Beliefs: The Spiritual Life of the Indus Valley Civilization...77
Chapter 9..**86**
The Mystery of the Vanishing Civilization................86
Chapter 10..**96**
Lessons from the Past: What We Can Learn from the Indus Valley Civilization...96

The Indus Valley Civilization

CHAPTER 1

The Mysterious Beginnings of the Indus Valley Civilization

Imagine a time long, long ago, when the world was very different from what we know today. The sun rose over the horizon, casting a warm golden glow on the banks of a mighty river. This river, called the Indus, flowed like a silver ribbon through a land filled with rich soil and lush greenery. It was here, around 2500 BCE, that a remarkable civilization began to flourish—the Indus Valley Civilization.

But who were the people of the Indus Valley? They were clever and skilled, creating one of the world's first urban societies. They built cities with straight streets and sturdy houses made of baked bricks, which were like building blocks of their own making. These cities, like Harappa and Mohenjo-Daro, were designed with great care. Picture a bustling marketplace where traders exchanged goods like spices, textiles, and beautiful jewelry. The air would have been filled with the sounds of laughter and chatter, as people went about their daily lives.

One of the most fascinating things about the Indus Valley Civilization is that they had a very advanced system of plumbing! Imagine having toilets in your home, just like we do today. The people of this civilization created a network of drains that carried waste away from their homes and into the streets. They even had public baths, where families could wash away the dust of the day. This shows us how important cleanliness and hygiene were to them, just as they are to us now.

As we explore the mysteries of this ancient civilization, we also wonder: how did they come to be? Historians believe that the people of the Indus Valley may have started as small farming communities. They grew crops like wheat and barley, and raised animals like cattle and sheep. Over time, these communities grew larger, and trade began to flourish. They exchanged goods not only with each other but also with distant lands, reaching as far as Mesopotamia. It's like a big cosmic web of connections, where each thread represents a trade route that brought different cultures together.

But here's the intriguing part: despite their achievements, the people of the Indus Valley left behind very few written records. They used a script that we still cannot fully understand, making it a puzzle for archaeologists and historians. It's as if they were whispering secrets to us from the past, and we are still trying to decode their messages. What were their dreams and hopes? What stories did they tell? These questions make us think deeply about the lives of those who came before us.

As we gaze upon the ruins of their cities, we can almost hear the echoes of laughter and conversation. We can picture children playing games in the streets, families gathering for meals, and traders haggling over the price of goods. The Indus Valley Civilization reminds us that people, no matter where or when they lived, shared many of the same joys and challenges that we experience today.

But what happened to this incredible civilization? Why did it fade away? Some believe that changes in climate, like droughts or floods, may have played a role. Others think that shifts in trade routes or conflicts with neighboring groups could have contributed to their decline. This mystery leaves us with a sense of wonder, urging us to think about how our actions today might affect the future of our own civilization.

As we close this chapter, let's take a moment to reflect on the lessons learned from the Indus Valley Civilization. They were a people who built a thriving society, valued cleanliness, and traded with others. Their story reminds us that, like them, we are all part of a larger tapestry woven through time, and our choices today can shape the world of tomorrow.

Key Takeaway: The Indus Valley Civilization teaches us the importance of community, innovation, and the mysteries of history. As we learn from the past, we can create a better future for ourselves and the world around us.

CHAPTER 2

Amazing Cities: The Urban Planning of Harappa and Mohenjo-Daro

Imagine stepping into a bustling city, where the streets are alive with the sounds of laughter, chatter, and the clinking of pottery. This city is not just any city; it's Harappa, one of the remarkable jewels of the ancient Indus Valley Civilization. As you walk through its well-planned streets, you can almost feel the heartbeat of a society that thrived thousands of years ago.

Harappa and its sister city, Mohenjo-Daro, were like the superheroes of urban planning in ancient times. They were built around 2500 BCE, long before many other famous cities we know today, like Rome or London. Imagine a place where the streets are so straight and organized that they look like a giant grid, just like a game of tic-tac-toe! The people of these cities had a special way of designing their homes and streets that made life easier and more comfortable.

Let's take a closer look at Harappa. Picture a city with houses made of sturdy baked bricks, which were much stronger than the mud houses that many people lived in back then. These houses were often two stories tall, with flat roofs where families could relax and enjoy the cool evening breeze. Can you imagine climbing up to the roof to gaze at the stars, feeling like you're touching the sky? Each house had its own courtyard, where families could gather and share stories, much like we do today around a dinner table.

Now, let's stroll through the streets of Mohenjo-Daro. The first thing you would notice is the impressive drainage system. Yes, you heard that right! The people of Mohenjo-Daro were like the architects of cleanliness. They built drains made of bricks that ran along the streets, carrying away rainwater and waste. This meant that the streets were not only tidy but also safe from floods. Imagine living in a city where you never had to worry about muddy streets after a rainstorm!

As you wander deeper into the city, you might stumble upon the Great Bath, a large public pool that was the pride of Mohenjo-Daro. It's like the city's own swimming pool, but even more special! This pool was used for bathing and possibly for important ceremonies. Picture people gathering around the pool, splashing water and laughing, while others sit on the steps, chatting and enjoying the sun. The Great Bath was a place of community, where everyone came together to celebrate life.

What's even more fascinating is how these cities were built with a deep understanding of nature. The people of Harappa and Mohenjo-Daro knew how to use the land and the rivers to their advantage. They built their cities near the Indus River, which provided them with water for drinking, cooking, and farming. Imagine the excitement of watching the river flow by, bringing life to the fields and the city!

But there's a mystery that surrounds these amazing cities. Why did they suddenly disappear around 1900 BCE? Some say it was because of climate changes, while others believe it was due to floods or even invasions. The truth remains hidden like a treasure buried deep in the sands of time. This mystery makes us wonder about the resilience of human life and how we adapt to challenges.

As we explore Harappa and Mohenjo-Daro, we can't help but reflect on our own cities today. How do we design our homes and streets? What can we learn from the ancient urban planners who built these incredible cities? The beauty of Harappa and Mohenjo-Daro is not just in their structures but in the way they remind us of our connection to the past and our responsibility for the future.

Key Takeaway: The cities of Harappa and Mohenjo-Daro teach us the importance of planning and caring for our environment. Just like them, we can create spaces that are not only beautiful but also safe and clean for everyone to enjoy.

The Indus Valley Civilization

Chapter 3

The Great Bath: An Ancient Wonder of Hygiene and Ritual

Once upon a time, in a land far away, there was a remarkable place known as the Indus Valley Civilization. This ancient society flourished over 4,500 years ago, and it was filled with wonders that still amaze us today. One of the most fascinating of these wonders is called the Great Bath, a huge, rectangular pool that was more than just a place to swim; it was a center of hygiene and ritual.

Imagine stepping into a bustling city like Mohenjo-Daro, where the streets were lined with mud-brick houses and the air was filled with the sounds of children playing and merchants selling their goods. As you walk through the city, you might notice a grand structure that stands out from the rest. It's the Great Bath, a magnificent pool that sparkles under the warm sun, inviting everyone to come closer.

The Great Bath was built with incredible skill, using baked bricks that fit together perfectly, just like pieces of a puzzle. Its walls were strong and sturdy, holding back the water that filled the pool. The pool itself was about 12 meters long and 7 meters wide, deep enough for people to wade in and splash around. Can you picture it? People laughing, children playing, and families gathering around this ancient wonder!

But the Great Bath was not just a place for fun. It had a deeper purpose, too. People in the Indus Valley believed in cleanliness and the importance of bathing. They thought that washing away dirt and sweat was not only good for the body but also for the spirit. Imagine the cool water washing over you, refreshing your skin and lifting your spirits, as if the water were a magical potion that cleansed you inside and out.

Now, picture this: a group of people dressed in beautiful clothes, their faces glowing with excitement, as they prepare for a special ceremony by the Great Bath. They would gather around the pool, offering flowers and lighting lamps, celebrating life and their connection to the divine. The Great Bath was a sacred place, where people came together not only to cleanse their bodies but also to cleanse their hearts and minds.

As we dive deeper into the history of the Great Bath, we learn that the people of the Indus Valley had a deep understanding of hygiene. They built sophisticated drainage systems and toilets in their homes, which were quite advanced for their time. Can you believe that they cared so much about cleanliness? This shows us that they valued health and well-being, just like we do today.

Imagine if we could visit the Great Bath in its prime, with the sun shining brightly and the air filled with laughter and joy. It would be a scene of happiness, where everyone came together to celebrate their culture and traditions. The Great Bath was more than just a pool; it was a symbol of community and connection, a place where friendships were formed and memories were made.

But let's take a moment to think about something important. Why is cleanliness so essential? Just like the people of the Indus Valley, we need to care for our bodies and our environment. When we keep ourselves clean, we feel good and healthy, ready to take on the world. And when we work together as a community to support each other, we create a happier and healthier place to live.

As we conclude our journey to the Great Bath, let's reflect on its significance. It was a place of hygiene, ritual, and community, reminding us that taking care of ourselves and our surroundings is vital. The Great Bath may have been built thousands of years ago, but its lessons still resonate with us today.

Key Takeaway: Cleanliness is important for our health and well-being, and when we come together as a community to support each other, we create a happier world. Just like the people of the Indus Valley, we can learn to value hygiene and the connections we share with one another.

THE INDUS VALLEY CIVILIZATION

Chapter 4

Writing Without Words: The Indus Script and Its Secrets

Imagine walking through a bustling ancient city, the sun shining brightly overhead. You hear the sounds of children laughing and merchants calling out their wares. As you stroll through the streets, you come across a mysterious wall covered in strange symbols. These symbols are part of the Indus Script, a writing system used by the people of the Indus Valley Civilization over 4,000 years ago! But here's the catch: no one knows exactly what these symbols mean.

The Indus Valley Civilization was one of the earliest urban societies in the world, flourishing along the banks of the Indus River in what is now Pakistan and northwest India. They built impressive cities like Harappa and Mohenjo-Daro, complete with advanced drainage systems and well-planned streets. But what makes this civilization truly fascinating is their unique way of communicating.

The Indus Script consists of more than 400 different symbols, some of which look like animals, while others resemble geometric shapes. Imagine trying to read a book filled with pictures instead of words! Some scholars believe these symbols might represent sounds, while others think they could be more like ideas or objects. It's like trying to solve a puzzle with missing pieces, and the excitement of discovery hangs in the air.

One day, a curious archaeologist named Sir Mortimer Wheeler decided to dig deeper into the mysteries of the Indus Script. He carefully examined the seals, small carved stones used for trade, that featured these symbols. Each seal told a story of its own, but without a key to unlock the secrets, Wheeler was left with more questions than answers. "What did these people want to say?" he wondered, his mind racing with possibilities.

Picture the seals: some showed animals like elephants and tigers, while others depicted strange human figures. These tiny artifacts were like windows into the past, offering glimpses of a world long gone. But despite their beauty, they held a secret that remained locked away, waiting for someone to discover the truth.

As time passed, many researchers attempted to decipher the Indus Script, but it remained stubbornly elusive. It's as if the people of the Indus Valley wanted to keep their stories just for themselves. Some believe they might have been writing about their daily lives, trade, or even religious beliefs. Imagine reading about a grand festival filled with music and dance, or a bustling market where people exchanged goods from faraway lands!

The mystery of the Indus Script invites us to ponder the power of communication. Why did these ancient people choose to write? What were they trying to express? Perhaps they wanted to connect with one another, share their dreams, or preserve their history for future generations. Just like how we write in our diaries or send messages to friends, they might have felt the need to share their thoughts and experiences.

As we explore this ancient writing, we also reflect on our own lives. We write stories, draw pictures, and create songs to share our feelings and ideas. The Indus Script reminds us that communication is a bridge connecting us to others, no matter how far apart we may be in time or space.

In a world where technology allows us to send messages in an instant, the Indus Script teaches us the value of patience and understanding. Just as we sometimes struggle to find the right words to express ourselves, the people of the Indus Valley faced their own challenges in sharing their thoughts. Their symbols may be silent, but they echo through time, inviting us to listen closely and imagine the stories they once told.

So, as we stand before the ancient seals and symbols of the Indus Valley, let's embrace the mystery and wonder they hold. Let's celebrate the beauty of communication, whether through words, symbols, or art. And let's remember that every time we share a story, we connect with the hearts and minds of those who came before us and those who will come after.

Key Takeaway: The Indus Script teaches us that communication is a powerful tool that connects us across time and space. Just like the people of the Indus Valley, we can express our thoughts and feelings in many different ways, reminding us of the importance of sharing our stories with the world.

THE INDUS VALLEY CIVILIZATION

Chapter 5

Trade and Travel: How the Indus Valley Connected the World

Imagine a bustling marketplace, filled with the sounds of laughter, the clinking of coins, and the delightful aromas of spices wafting through the air. This lively scene was not just a dream; it was the everyday reality of the

Indus Valley Civilization, a remarkable society that thrived thousands of years ago. Stretching across what is now modern-day Pakistan and northwest India, the Indus Valley was a vibrant hub of trade and travel, connecting people from far and wide.

Picture the ancient city of Mohenjo-Daro, where the streets were lined with sturdy brick houses and the sun shone brightly overhead. Merchants and traders from different regions gathered here, eager to exchange their goods. They brought precious items like beautiful beads made from lapis lazuli, a deep blue stone that sparkled like the night sky. Imagine children's eyes lighting up as they gazed at the shimmering treasures, dreaming of the adventures that lay beyond their city walls.

But how did the people of the Indus Valley become such skilled traders? The answer lies in their unique location. Nestled between the towering Himalayas to the north and the vast Arabian Sea to the south, the Indus Valley was perfectly positioned for trade. It was like a bridge connecting the rich lands of Mesopotamia to the bustling markets of the Persian Gulf. This strategic spot allowed the

Indus Valley people to share their goods with distant lands, making them important players in the ancient world.

One of the most exciting aspects of trade in the Indus Valley was the variety of goods exchanged. Imagine a colorful tapestry of cultures woven together through the marketplace. Traders from Mesopotamia brought barley and wool, while those from the Arabian Peninsula offered exotic spices and precious metals. The Indus Valley people, in turn, shared their unique products, like cotton textiles that were soft and colorful, and pottery adorned with intricate designs. This exchange of goods not only enriched their lives but also helped them learn about different cultures and traditions.

But trade wasn't just about exchanging items; it was also about building friendships and connections. Picture a trader named Ravi, who traveled from Mohenjo-Daro to a distant land. As he journeyed along the banks of the Indus River, he met people from different cultures. They shared stories, laughter, and even meals together, creating bonds that transcended borders. Ravi returned home with more than just goods; he brought back tales of adventure and friendship, reminding everyone that the world was much bigger than they had ever imagined.

The Indus Valley people were also skilled navigators. They didn't just rely on land routes; they took to the waters, sailing along rivers and the coastlines. Imagine sturdy wooden boats gliding across the shimmering waves, carrying precious cargo to far-off lands. The sailors would have felt the salty breeze on their faces, their hearts racing with excitement as they explored the unknown.

This spirit of adventure and curiosity drove them to discover new places and meet new people, expanding their horizons and enriching their lives.

As the Indus Valley Civilization flourished, so did their influence on the world. They created a network of trade routes that extended beyond their borders, reaching as far as Egypt and Mesopotamia. Imagine the thrill of receiving goods from distant lands, each item telling a story of its journey. The exchange of ideas, art, and culture flowed like a river, shaping the lives of people across the ancient world.

However, with great trade came great responsibility. The Indus Valley people understood that their actions had consequences. They recognized the importance of protecting their environment and resources. Just as a gardener tends to a delicate flower, they cared for their land, ensuring that it would thrive for generations to come. They knew that their success as traders depended on the health of their surroundings, and they worked hard to be good stewards of the earth.

As we ponder the legacy of the Indus Valley Civilization, we can't help but ask ourselves: How do we connect with the world around us today? In a time when we can communicate with anyone across the globe at the click of a button, we must remember the lessons of the past. The Indus Valley people showed us that trade and travel are not just about exchanging goods; they are about building relationships, understanding different cultures, and caring for our planet.

Key Takeaway: The Indus Valley Civilization teaches us the importance of connecting with others, sharing our resources, and being responsible stewards of the earth as we explore the world around us.

Chapter 6

The Art of Living: Crafts, Jewelry, and Toys of the Indus People

Imagine stepping into a bustling marketplace over 4,000 years ago, where the air is filled with the scent of spices and the sound of laughter. You're in the heart of the

Indus Valley Civilization, a remarkable society that thrived along the banks of the Indus River in what is now Pakistan and northwest India. Here, the people didn't just focus on farming and trade; they also created beautiful crafts, stunning jewelry, and delightful toys that brought joy to their lives.

As you wander through the marketplace, your eyes are drawn to colorful pottery that sparkles in the sunlight. The Indus people were master potters, skillfully shaping clay into bowls, jars, and figurines. Some of these pots were painted with intricate designs, showcasing animals, flowers, and geometric patterns. Each piece tells a story, reflecting the creativity and artistic flair of its maker. Can you imagine the joy of holding a pot that was crafted by someone's hands so long ago?

But it wasn't just pottery that captured the imagination of the Indus people. They were also talented jewelers, creating exquisite ornaments that adorned their bodies. Picture a young girl named Maya, who loved to wear her mother's beautiful necklace made of colorful beads and shimmering gold. The Indus jewelers used materials like gold, silver, and semi-precious stones, carefully crafting earrings, bracelets, and necklaces that sparkled like stars in the night sky. Each piece of jewelry was not just an accessory; it was a symbol of beauty and status, connecting the wearer to their family and community.

Now, let's take a moment to think about the toys that brought laughter and excitement to the children of the Indus Valley. Imagine a little boy named Arjun, playing with a small clay cart pulled by tiny animal figurines. The Indus people crafted toys that were not only fun but also educational, helping children learn about their world. Some toys even resembled real animals, like cows and elephants, and were painted in bright colors. Can you picture Arjun racing his cart down a dusty street, his laughter echoing through the air?

The creativity of the Indus people didn't stop at crafts and toys. They also created intricate seals, small stone carvings that were used to mark goods and trade. These seals often featured animals, like unicorns and tigers, and symbols that we still don't fully understand today. It's as if the Indus people left behind a secret code, inviting us to unlock the mysteries of their civilization.

As we explore the art of living in the Indus Valley, we can see how their crafts, jewelry, and toys were not just objects; they were a reflection of their culture, beliefs, and everyday life. Each creation tells us something about who they were as a people. They celebrated beauty, shared joy, and connected with one another through their art.

Now, let's ponder a big question: How does creativity shape our lives today? Just like the Indus people, we express ourselves through art, music, and play. What stories do our creations tell about us?

In this vibrant world of the Indus Valley, we learn that art is not just about making things; it's about connecting with others, celebrating life, and expressing who we are.

Key Takeaway: The crafts, jewelry, and toys of the Indus people remind us that creativity is a powerful way to express ourselves and connect with our communities. What will you create to tell your story?

Chapter 7

Farming Innovations: The Agricultural Techniques of the Indus Valley

Once upon a time, in a land where the mighty rivers flowed and the sun painted the skies in hues of orange and gold, there thrived a remarkable civilization known as the Indus

Valley Civilization. This ancient society, which flourished around 2500 BCE, was like a giant garden filled with vibrant crops and bustling farmers. Imagine walking through their fields, where the air is filled with the sweet scent of ripe wheat and the sound of rustling leaves dances in the gentle breeze.

The farmers of the Indus Valley were not just any farmers; they were innovators! They had a magical connection with the land and a deep understanding of how to grow food. They cultivated various crops, including wheat, barley, peas, and even cotton. But how did they do it? Let's explore the secrets of their farming techniques!

First, picture a farmer named Ravi, standing proudly in his field. He looked up at the sky and noticed the dark clouds gathering. Instead of worrying about the rain, he smiled, for he knew that the rivers nearby would soon swell with water, nourishing his crops. The Indus Valley was blessed with the Indus River and its tributaries, which provided a steady supply of water. The farmers ingeniously used this water by creating a system of canals. These canals acted like tiny rivers, guiding water right to their fields. It was like they had their own magical waterway, helping their crops grow strong and healthy!

But that's not all! The Indus Valley farmers also practiced a technique called crop rotation. Imagine planting different crops in the same field each year, like a game of musical chairs for plants! This method kept the soil rich and full of nutrients, ensuring that the farmers could harvest bountiful crops year after year. Ravi might plant wheat one season, then switch to barley the next. This clever trick helped keep the soil happy and productive.

And let's not forget about the tools they used! The farmers crafted simple yet effective tools from stone and metal. They had plows to till the soil, making it soft and ready for planting. Picture Ravi as he skillfully guided his plow through the earth, turning it over like flipping pancakes. With every turn, he prepared the ground for the seeds that would soon sprout into life.

Now, close your eyes and imagine the scene: golden fields stretching as far as the eye can see, with farmers working side by side under the warm sun. The laughter of children echoes in the background as they chase butterflies and help their parents gather the harvest. It was a time of community and togetherness, where everyone played a part in the circle of life.

But what made the Indus Valley farmers truly special was their respect for nature. They understood that the earth was a living being, and they treated it with care. They didn't just take; they gave back to the land. By using compost made from leftover plants and animal waste, they enriched the soil, creating a cycle of growth that benefited both the crops and the environment. It was as if they were in a beautiful dance with nature, moving in harmony with the rhythms of the earth.

As we think about the innovations of the Indus Valley farmers, we might wonder: What can we learn from their wisdom? In our fast-paced world, where we often forget to appreciate the beauty of nature, these ancient farmers remind us of the importance of caring for our planet. Just like Ravi and his friends, we too can make choices that help our environment thrive.

Key Takeaway: The farmers of the Indus Valley Civilization taught us that by working with nature and respecting the earth, we can grow not only food but also a brighter future for ourselves and the planet. How can we apply their lessons in our own lives today?

The Indus Valley Civilization

CHAPTER 8

Religion and Beliefs: The Spiritual Life of the Indus Valley Civilization

In the heart of the ancient Indus Valley Civilization, nestled between the mighty rivers of the Indus and the Ghaggar-Hakra, lay a world brimming with mystery and wonder. Imagine walking through the bustling streets of Harappa or Mohenjo-Daro, where the air is filled with the sounds of merchants calling out their wares and children laughing as they play. But beyond the everyday life of these people, there was something deeper—an intricate web of beliefs and spirituality that colored their existence.

The people of the Indus Valley were not just builders of cities; they were seekers of meaning. They looked up at the stars twinkling in the night sky and wondered about the forces that governed their lives. Who controlled the rain that nourished their crops? What lay beyond the horizon? These questions led them to develop a rich tapestry of religious beliefs.

Archaeologists have uncovered evidence of small figurines and seals that suggest the Indus people worshipped a variety of deities. One of the most famous is the "Priest-King" statue, a figure that seems to radiate authority and serenity. Was he a leader, a priest, or perhaps a bridge between the people and the divine? The mysteries of his identity echo through time, inviting us to ponder the significance of leadership in their spiritual life.

Picture a scene where families gather around their clay hearths, sharing stories of gods and goddesses. The Indus Valley people believed in powerful forces that could bring prosperity or disaster. They worshipped nature—goddesses of fertility, animals like the bull, and the sacred tree. The bull, for instance, was a symbol of strength and fertility, often depicted in their art. Children would hear tales of how the goddess of the harvest blessed their fields, ensuring that they would have enough food to eat.

But it wasn't just about worship; it was also about connection. The Indus Valley people believed in a cosmic balance, where every action had a reaction. They understood that their relationship with nature and the divine was a dance, much like the graceful movements of a ballet. If they honored the gods, the gods would, in turn, bless them with bountiful harvests and happy lives. This interdependence is a beautiful reminder that we, too, are part of a larger story, connected to the world around us.

As the sun dipped below the horizon, casting a golden glow over the ancient cities, rituals filled the air with a sense of reverence. They would light oil lamps and offer flowers and fruits to their deities, creating a fragrant atmosphere of devotion. Imagine the flickering flames casting shadows on the walls, as the people whispered prayers and hopes into the night.

However, not everything was peaceful in the spiritual life of the Indus Valley. There were challenges and uncertainties, much like the storms that sometimes swept through their lands. The people faced droughts, floods, and other natural disasters that tested their faith. How did they cope with such challenges? They turned to their beliefs, finding strength in the idea that the divine was always watching over them, guiding them through the darkness.

But as we explore their beliefs, we must also ask ourselves—what can we learn from the Indus Valley Civilization? How can their spirituality guide us in our own lives? Just like them, we seek answers to big questions. Why are we here? How can we live in harmony with nature? The Indus people remind us of the importance of respect, gratitude, and connection to the world around us.

As we delve deeper into the mysteries of the Indus Valley, we realize that their spiritual life was not just about rituals and deities; it was about understanding their place in the universe. They were part of a grand cosmic story, just like we are today.

Key Takeaway: The spiritual life of the Indus Valley Civilization teaches us the importance of connection—to each other, to nature, and to the mysteries of the universe. Just as they sought meaning in their beliefs, we too can find strength and purpose in understanding our place in the world.

Chapter 9

The Mystery of the Vanishing Civilization

Imagine standing on the banks of a great river, the Indus River, where once stood a bustling city filled with life and laughter. This city, part of the Indus Valley Civilization, was a marvel of its time, with streets laid out in perfect grids and houses made of baked bricks. But as the sun set over this ancient land, something mysterious happened. The vibrant civilization began to fade away, like a beautiful painting washed away by rain.

What happened to the people of the Indus Valley? This is a question that has puzzled historians and archaeologists for centuries. As we explore this mystery, let's picture ourselves as detectives, piecing together clues from the past.

The Indus Valley Civilization

The Indus Valley Civilization flourished around 2500 BCE, a time when people lived in harmony with nature. They were skilled farmers, growing wheat, barley, and cotton. They even made beautiful jewelry and pottery! Their cities, like Harappa and Mohenjo-Daro, were filled with impressive buildings and advanced drainage systems. It was like a magical kingdom where everything seemed perfect.

But then, around 1900 BCE, something changed. The cities began to crumble, and the people vanished. It's as if they had packed their bags and disappeared into thin air! What could have caused such a sudden change?

One of the leading theories is that climate change played a significant role. Imagine a giant blanket of clouds covering the sun, making the land dry and dusty. The rivers that once flowed abundantly might have shrunk, making it hard for the farmers to grow their crops. Without food, the people would have had to leave their homes in search of greener pastures.

But that's not the only possibility. Some researchers believe that natural disasters, like earthquakes, could have shaken the very foundations of their cities. Picture the ground trembling beneath your feet, buildings collapsing like a house of cards. This could have frightened the people and forced them to abandon their beloved homes.

Then there's the idea of conflict. Just like in a thrilling adventure story, rival groups may have fought for resources like water and land. Imagine brave warriors clashing in the streets, the sounds of battle echoing through the once-peaceful city. In the end, the people might have felt they had no choice but to leave, seeking safety elsewhere.

As we dive deeper into this mystery, we find ourselves pondering the fate of these ancient people. Where did they go? Did they blend into other cultures, or did they simply vanish into the pages of history? It's a riddle that invites us to think about our own lives. Just as the Indus Valley Civilization faced challenges, we too face obstacles in our world today. How do we respond to changes around us? Are we adaptable like the ancient people, finding new ways to thrive?

The story of the Indus Valley Civilization is not just about what happened long ago; it's a reflection of our own journey through life. As we look up at the stars and wonder about our place in the universe, we can learn from the past. The rise and fall of civilizations remind us that change is a part of life, and how we respond to it shapes our future.

So, as we leave the mystery of the vanishing civilization behind, let's carry its lessons with us. The beauty of the Indus Valley Civilization may have faded, but its story continues to inspire us to explore, adapt, and cherish the world we live in.

Key Takeaway: The mystery of the Indus Valley Civilization teaches us that change is a natural part of life. Just like the ancient people faced challenges, we too can learn to adapt and find new ways to thrive in our ever-changing world.

The Indus Valley Civilization

CHAPTER 10

Lessons from the Past: What We Can Learn from the Indus Valley Civilization

Once upon a time, in a land far away, there was a thriving civilization known as the Indus

Valley Civilization. It flourished over 4,500 years ago in what is now Pakistan and northwest India. Imagine walking through the bustling streets of Harappa or Mohenjo-Daro, where the sun casts golden rays over well-planned homes and vibrant marketplaces. The air is filled with the chatter of merchants selling colorful pottery, and children play games that echo through the narrow lanes. But beyond this lively scene, there are valuable lessons hidden in the ruins of this ancient society.

The people of the Indus Valley were master builders. They constructed cities with straight streets, advanced drainage systems, and sturdy brick houses. Picture a city where every home has a bathroom, and waste flows away cleanly through underground pipes. This was a remarkable achievement for their time! Their careful planning shows us the importance of organization and teamwork. Just like the Indus Valley people worked together to create their cities, we can learn to collaborate in our own communities to make them better places to live.

But what about their farming? The Indus Valley Civilization thrived because of its rich agricultural practices. Farmers grew wheat, barley, and cotton, feeding their families and trading surplus crops with others. Imagine vast fields of golden grains swaying in the breeze, as farmers tend to their crops with love and care. This teaches us the significance of sustainability. If we take good care of our planet, just like the farmers of the Indus Valley did, we can ensure that future generations have enough food and resources to thrive.

Yet, even the most successful civilizations face challenges. The Indus Valley Civilization mysteriously declined around 1900 BCE. Some historians believe it was due to climate change, which may have caused rivers to dry up, making it difficult to farm. Others suggest that trade disruptions or invasions played a role. This part of their story invites us to reflect on our own actions. Are we taking care of our environment? Are we prepared for changes that could affect our lives? The rise and fall of the Indus Valley Civilization remind us that we must be responsible stewards of our planet and work together to overcome challenges.

As we ponder the lessons from the Indus Valley, we can also think about their writing system, which remains a mystery. They used symbols to communicate, but we have yet to fully understand what they meant. This sparks curiosity! It teaches us the importance of communication and learning from one another. Just as the Indus Valley people sought to express their thoughts, we should strive to share our ideas and listen to others. Who knows what wonders we might uncover when we come together to share our knowledge?

The story of the Indus Valley Civilization is not just about the past; it is a mirror reflecting our present and future. We can learn to build better communities, protect our environment, and communicate effectively. Each lesson they left behind is like a treasure waiting to be discovered, urging us to be better caretakers of our world.

So, as you gaze up at the stars, remember the lessons of the Indus Valley. Imagine a world where we all work together, just like those ancient builders, farmers, and thinkers.

What kind of future could we create if we learned from the past?

Key Takeaway: The Indus Valley Civilization teaches us the importance of teamwork, sustainability, and communication. By learning from their successes and challenges, we can build a better world for ourselves and future generations.

Dear Cool Kids/Parents

Thank you for choosing "What the History"! We hope this book has ignited a spark of wonder and motivation within you.

If you found this book captivating and believe in the transformative power of its message, we kindly ask for your support. Please consider leaving a glowing review on the platform where you purchased the book. Your review will help spread this message of empowerment to even more young readers, inspiring them to dream big and reach for the stars.

The core essence of this book - to inspire and uplift young minds - is what truly matters. We acknowledge that perfection is elusive, and we appreciate your understanding and forgiveness for any minor imperfections.

Thank you for being a part of our mission to nurture the brilliance and potential within the next generation. Your feedback will go a long way in helping us continue to provide captivating and transformative stories for young readers.

The Indus Valley Civilization

Printed in Great Britain
by Amazon